Moon Child

Yentl Muit

BookLeaf
Publishing

India | USA | UK

Presentation by *BookLeaf Publishing*

Web: www.bookleafpub.com

E-mail: info@bookleafpub.com

ISBN: 978-93-5744-974-8

First edition 2022

DEDICATION

To Isabel,

For all your love and encouragement

Forever

I think it's funny how both of us
Forgot when it has begun exactly
As if when we said "friends forever"
We really were always meant to be

Runaways

Shall we escape, get away from this place?
Run away from this reality that's our life
To live careless and have fun together
Enjoy the youth we were never given
For we were children in a harsh world

Show me the world through your eyes
Show me the possibilities of the future
Learn me how to wonder like you do
Let's forget about the stories of the past
Tell me all about your buried dreams

I look at the unknown and smile
I know the future isn't scary, but bright
There's a guidelight in the darkness
We'll wander and build our home
And the sun will shine on us again

Compass

It doesn't matter where we are
I'll be looking to see if you're near
Happily admiring you telling stories
With those sparkles in your eyes

I'll follow you wherever you go
Through historical old villages
And the crowds of lively cities
You'll always be my true north

Here comes the goddess

The winter parted its way for her
As the sun rose up like her spotlight
And the wind announced her coming
'Behold, here comes the goddess'

With a touch of her hand she brought back
The stunning beauty there once was in wealth
Flowers came back to life and rose once again
'This, this is the work of a goddess'

Humans looked and tried to find her
But only found the life she left behind
The spring that showed her presence
'Look, the goddess was really here'

The world became brighter with a simple smile
And deep inside his bones, the god felt alive
Losing sense of time as she awoke the dead
'Persephone, the goddess of spring'

Dear earth - part I

Dear earth,
Do you still bottle up your powers?
Waiting to show us all your colors?
Do you still feel safe with us people?

Dear trees,
Do you like standing still and watch us grow?
Wishing that we'll come play outside again?
Do you like being useful to us even if it hurts?

Dear wind,
Do you hear the people cry of joy?
Whispering that we should cherish it?
Do you hear the people cry of sadness?

Dear stars,
Do you see the explosions of fireworks?
Wondering if you could be as beautiful?
Do you see the explosions of bombs?

Dear earth - part II

Dear earth,
I can't hear you scream in my language
But maybe in the people you never left
You're still here after all these years

You're all around me, I can see it now
I can try to help you a little, tell me how
Hey, stay with me alright? You'll be okay

Please, I don't want to be deaf anymore

Your future

You focus so much on the future
Because one day you'll live there
With everything you've prepared for
With everything like you wanted it to be

A dream turned into a goal
Sacrifices made for the better
Your ideals will make it worth it
I can only watch and learn from you

Look up at the stars and listen to me
You were always enough to be alive
Without waiting, without conditions
Just exist with me in this moment

Your passion and dedication make me wonder
What does the future have what the present
doesn't?
Is it the fulfillment of your destiny, is this not
enough?

Moving on

We're over now, with no way back
You're forgiven, free to move on
I don't need your late apologies
Make peace with your regrets
We can part ways and make space
To heal and to be better to others
To be who we were meant to be

Without you

I still opened my mouth
To say what's on my mind
Hoping on your reaction
Before I realized that
You're no longer here
Nobody is next to me
Only me without you
Like it was before

Too much

You won't ever be "too much"
If you learn how to love yourself
As much as you have loved others
You deserve good things in life
To give and receive in return
Let yourself be loved again
Break down your walls
And let in the light

Star

A new environment, new chances, a new you
The weight on your shoulders, the spotlight
upon you
Maybe this is your time to shine, you have to try
To prove everyone that you can be better once
more
That you can breakdown and build up all on
your own
The place where you belong has always been on
top
Everyone knows that, everyone keeps telling
you so

Perfectionism

'If you truly care, you would do better,' a voice
said
I become happy and hopeful, then overwhelmed
and anxious
Looking for proof that this time I won't waste
the opportunity

'It gives you direction, but it's just an illusion,' I
learnt
I got exhausted from needing validation, because
I still felt empty
I got lost from wanting things, because I learnt
how to live without it

'It'll be worth it, just do your best,' a voice said
I don't have to proof myself, but I want to be
wanted and loved
I want it to be over quickly, but I want to
deserve good things and rest

'It gives you hope before it tears you down,' I
learnt
Maybe if I can fake it long enough everything
will turn out fine eventually

Forms of love

I know that they loved me
They loved me in their own ways
Maybe different from how I wanted
But with good intentions deep within

I liked how all the love languages
Showed a little different in all of them
But later I saw how some gestures of love
Got lost in translation and wrong perception

And as I grew up I realized that love hurts too
That sometimes good intentions aren't enough
Sometimes we don't grow from what we get
And break into a thousand pieces instead

No matter how much it felt like a fairy tale
I came to terms that some of the actions
Maybe never were a form of love at all
True love doesn't go together with fear

Warnings

You showed me that people could be good
Warned me about how cruel the world could be
I tried to listen, to remember all you've said
I'm trying to be happy, while keeping your
warnings in mind

You make it sound like I'm worthy of having
fears
Convincing me that I would get chosen as victim
Then getting annoyed that I'm not living life
more
That I'm not doing the stupid things others
teenagers do

I'll figure out myself how to be happy and on
guard
Experience how good and bad people can be in
life
Discussing all possibilities and intentions in my
mind
As if I want to admit that you might've been
right, even late

To be honest

Fear my power when I've outgrown you
I'll start talking back when you treat me wrong
I'm not afraid anymore, I can protect myself
now
I can afford it to be honest, to show you all my
feelings

You're going to have to stop projecting and see
for yourself
We can both be hurt and angry, while both being
wrong
Hurting each other doesn't have to make us bad
people
Stop being scared of that, be responsible for
what you said

The truth will set you free

The truth will set you free
From all your pain and regrets
But not until it's done with you
And has torn down all your lies
When you'll see for yourself that
All your lies were as fragile as you
And that nothing is meant to last forever

Are you happy too?

Hey, I got the news: I did it
I couldn't believe it at first
My anxiety finally disappears
Pride and happiness fill me
It feels so good to be happy

I'll tell you about it, I promise
You'll probably be happier than me
So I'll just sit here for a little longer
And celebrate my own feelings
Without adaptation or projection

So when you'll ask "are you happy too?"
I'll know that it was worth it
To do something for myself

Endings

Everything has a beginning and an ending
Time does it for us or we do it by choice
I still light up whenever I talk about you
Even though it ended and I'm on my own

As we grew up together I saw it happen
Our souls were intertwined with each other
But our futures had different things in store
We slowly started letting go and grew apart

I cherish all of our adventures as we part
I move on in peace, grateful for everything
I'm happy that you were a part of my story
But now a new chapter is awaiting to begin

www.ingramcontent.com/pod-product-compliance
Lightning Source LLC
La Vergne TN
LVHW050310200726
843509LV00015B/3261